EVERYBODY'S CURIOUS ABOUT THE FUTURE

The unprecedented waves of people seeking information about the future from prophets and prophetesses, fortune tellers, astrologers, and spiritualistic mediums is just one sign of our anxiety about tomorrow.

But where to go for really reliable information? Doug Chatham suggests we try the Bible. He's convinced that everything we need to know about the future is right there. And the wealth of information he comes up with is truly impressive. . . .

The Rapture Book

by Doug Chatham

Whitaker House

ISBN: 0–88368–046–7

WHITAKER HOUSE
504 Laurel Drive
Monroeville, Pennsylvania 15146
(412) 372–6420

Printed in the United States of America

CONTENTS

FOREWORD

In her book, TRAMP FOR THE LORD, Corrie ten Boom tells of speaking before a group of young theologians on the Second Coming of Christ. A brash young theolog challenged her. "For 2000 years Christians have believed this myth. Can't you understand all this talk is nonsense?"

Tante Corrie, a stubborn old Dutch woman in her eighties, smiled and said, "Thank you, young man, for proving that Jesus is coming in this generation. The Bible says the generation who shall see His return shall hear scoffers such as you. You, my young friend, are one of the 'signs of the times'."

Another sign, according to the Bible, will be a new outpouring of the Holy Spirit on all flesh. Doug Chatham is one of God's new breed, called out to minister to the Body of Christ. A Spirit-baptized Southern Baptist, he is not only preparing his Atlanta flock for the Second Coming, but in this book is urging the rest of us to make ready also.

Regardless of the many interpretations of "end-time Scriptures," all Spirit-baptized people seem to agree definitely on one point: He *is* returning—soon.

There is a new expectancy in the air as ears are being cocked to hear the sound of the trumpet. The Church is coming into holiness, as a bride waiting for her husband. Doug's book is like a tuning fork, sounding the key for the blast of the trumpet which will soon be heard.

Jamie Buckingham
Melbourne, Florida

PREFACE

Prophecy, or prediction of future events, occupies approximately one quarter of all the Bible. The major subject of prophecy in the Bible is the Second Coming of our Lord. It is dealt with 1,845 times. Of these, 318 are in the New Testament. The Second Coming is the dominant theme of seventeen Old Testament books and one letter in the New Testament. Seven out of every ten chapters in the New Testament make some reference to the Second Coming! By sheer weight, the doctrine of the Second Coming demands the attention of every student of God's Word, and of every Christian who lives with this hope.

Out of the whole glorious spectrum of the scriptural picture of the Second Coming, the brightest spot to the eye of the believer is the event known as the Rapture. It is the most immediate prospect to the Christians living in this dispensation, called in the Scriptures the "fulness of the Gentiles" (Romans 11:25).

For the most part, the numerous prophecies mentioned above deal with other events and conditions relating to the Second Coming; some of the events are shown on the chart on page 22. Some of the prophetic subjects included under the general title, "Second Coming," are: (1) The appearance of Christ with the armies of heaven to victoriously conclude the Battle of Armageddon (Zechariah 14:1–5); (2) The judgment of nations (Matthew 25:31–36; Acts 17:31; 2 Thessalonians 1:7–10); (3) Our Lord's visible return to the same Mount of Olives from which He ascended, and the establishment of Jerusalem as the location of His throne and the seat of His government (Zechariah 14:4, 9, 16; Revelation 11:15; Isaiah 59:20; 60:14; Revelation 1:7), beginning the reign of Christ and the saints for a thousand years on the earth (Revelation 20:4–6; 2:26; Jude 14, 15; 1 Corinthians 6:2); (4) The loosing and destruction of Satan (Revelation 20:7–10); (5) The destruction of the present heavens and earth (2 Peter 3:10–13; Revelation 20:11; 21:1), and the end of time (Revelation 10:5, 6); (6) The Judgement of the Great White Throne (Revelation 20:11–15).

The single event of the Rapture or "catching up" of the Church into heaven will precede all the above events. The Scriptures clearly indicate this as a separate, distinct part of the great drama of the "Day of the Lord." (Study 1 Thessalonians 4:13–17; 1 Corinthians 15:51–54; Philippians 3:20, 21; John 14:1–3; Revelation 19:7–9; Luke 17:30–36).

It is my firm conviction that we are living in the "last days" which figure so prominently in prophecy, and which are to immediately precede the Rapture. We are not alone in this conviction. Millions of believers around the world are convinced that current events, predicted ages ago by the prophets of Israel, have moved us to the very threshold of the Rapture. This little book points to evidences of the Rapture's nearness, and describes in the light of Scripture the exciting details of this grand climax of the Christian Gospel.

INTRODUCTION

Doug Chatham offers you a manual by which you may study what the Bible teaches about the Rapture in the context of its general teaching about the Second Coming of Christ. Study this with your open Bible. You will *learn of* and *yearn for* our Lord's return for His saints. The book comes from a pastor's heart and experience.

Robert G. Witty, Th.D., Ph.D.
President, Luther Rice Seminary
Jacksonville, Florida

1 | What Happens During the Rapture?

TRANSFORMED!

The planet-wide phenomenon of the Rapture will be over in the "twinkling of an eye" (1 Corinthians 15:51–52). All the bodies of born-again Christians in all the cemeteries in all the nations on all the continents will be brought forth from their ripped-open graves. Also, all the Christian believers *living* on this entire globe will have their bodies instantly transformed into spectacular glory like those shooting up out of the graves. Upon being transformed, we will swish suddenly into the air and, to our amazement, discover those we thought

13

dead in Christ sweeping up along with us into the sky. There, shining and magnificent, all of us will see Jesus and fix our gaze on the King of Kings (1 Thessalonians 4:14–17).

TRANSFERRED!

Faster than the speed of light—indeed, without any sensation of time, we will find ourselves "caught up" to heaven (compare 2 Corinthians 12:2, 4). This will be that very place where God dwells—the "third heaven"—not the cloudy heaven, not the starry heaven, but the third heaven which is the Paradise Jesus promised the dying thief. Since we know that Jesus promised the repentant and believing thief that he would that same day be with Him in Paradise, we know that many of the dead in Christ will already be acquainted with the unspeakable beauty of that place. During the time of waiting for the Rapture, to be absent from the body is to be present with the Lord (2 Corinthians 5:8; Philippians 1:23).

CELESTIAL BODIES EXCHANGED FOR RESURRECTION BODIES

And that brings up a very wonderful fact: *those souls* whose *bodies* "sleep in Jesus" will be brought with Him when He comes (1 Thessalonians 4:14). This means that when we bury the body of a dead one in Christ, his soul is already with Christ in heaven (Philippians 1:23; Luke 23:43)!

Nor does that soul suffer the absence of a body while waiting in heaven for the Rapture. According to 2 Corinthians 5:1-3, as soon as we find ourselves unclothed from our mortal bodies in physical death, we immediately discover ourselves housed in heavenly bodies that are convenient counterparts to those we have just vacated. The example of the heavenly body of Moses, which appeared in the Transfiguration event (Luke 9:30-32), helps us be sure of this comforting thought. (Also, the story of the rich man and Lazarus, in Luke 16, indicates that those who die out of Christ immediately suffer physical sensations in a "counterpart body" in hell.)

As perfect as these celestial bodies are (1 Corinthians 15:40)—for nothing will ever enter heaven that is not perfect—these souls who now wait in heaven joyfully expect an even more wonderful Resurrection body! God's sure Word tells us that the earthly bodies of believers will be re-fashioned during the Resurrection. And the new image will be in the likeness of Christ Himself (Philippians 3:21; 1 Corinthians 15:49; Romans 8:29; 1 John 3:2). What a glorious prospect!

So the saints in heaven, sweeping down through the universe with Christ in that sudden but long awaited moment, will be coming to be clothed in the glory of the likeness of Christ. Paul reminds us in 1 Corinthians 15:51 that not all of our bodies will "sleep." Some of us will still be living when the Resurrection takes place. But we shall experience that same change (1 Corinthians 15:51–54), and be conformed to the image of Christ like all other believers (Romans 8:29).

This grand and glorious movement—Christ and the saints swooping down from outer space to catch up every resurrected body and every transformed believer, and their disappearance from this entire universe—will all take place in the twinkling of an eye!

A SPACE TRIP

Try to imagine what it would be like to experience what Enoch experienced (Hebrews 11:5; Genesis 5:22): To be going about everyday business—to be caught away in a flash by something like the whirlwind that caught away Elijah (2 Kings 2:1, 11)—to see the earth disappearing as a small speck in the distance behind you—to see also that the sun, the solar system, the galaxies and the whole universe have all as quickly disappeared from view! What a space trip! And what speed!

We will not be mere astronauts, nor even cosmonauts; we will be heaven-nauts!

OTHERS LEFT BEHIND

Now try to imagine the situation among the non-believers in the moment of the Rapture. Left behind! That is the tragedy. "For what is a man profited, if he shall gain the whole world, and lose his own soul?" (Matthew 16:26). What a terrible, terrible tragedy! After repeatedly hearing God's offer of free salvation, think how many will have refused it, and in that moment be forever left out.

So much happening in the twinkling of an eye! Millions of believers will disappear, more millions of believers' graves will open, and yet more millions of lost souls will remain exactly where they happen to be at the moment, doing what they happen to be doing.

LISTEN FOR THESE SOUNDS!

"Throughout the Scriptures, we are told repeatedly that the coming of Christ will be accompanied by the sound of a trumpet. A physics laboratory in upper New York has demonstrated that a large steel ball can be hoisted and held aloft in mid-air by focusing an intense beam of high frequency sound waves under the ball! The ultrasonic sound was too high a frequency to be detected by the human ear. This electronic phenomenon is the kind of thing that could happen when Christ returns to rapture (Latin, "to snatch away") His Church into the celestial. Those whose faith is in Christ, alive or deceased, will hear and respond to the trumpet call. To those without faith, the only realization will be that true believers are suddenly gone!" [1]

As a believer, however, I am excited at the prospect of hearing the shout of the Lord (1 Thessalonians 4:16) as He commands the dead, "Come forth!" Once before, He spoke "with a loud voice" (John 11:43), saying, "Lazarus, come forth." Augustine reasoned that Jesus called Lazarus by name in order to limit the resurrection to one man at that time. But on that great day, He will simply say, "Come forth!" And all those who know His voice (John 10:3) and hear that shout will come forth from their graves (John 5:25–28).

WHAT ABOUT FAITH?

At any moment we may hear the trumpet call of God, the shout of the Lord, and the voice of

1. White, John Wesley. *Re-entry*, p. 37.

the archangel (1 Thessalonians 4:16), and with our angelic escort soar away to be with the Lord. "Therefore be ye also ready: for in such an hour as ye think not the Son of man cometh" (Matthew 24:44). So be ready!

But Jesus posed this question: "When the Son of man cometh, shall he find faith on the earth?" (Luke 18:8). It will be the power of faith in Christ that will make us "blast off" in the Rapture. John Wesley White said, "It took 7,500,000 pounds of thrust (the power of 500 jet fighter planes) to get a Saturn V rocket with an Apollo aboard off its Florida launching pad en route to the moon. Is it not logical to believe that "when the Son of man cometh," the faith He shall find in the hearts of believers will far exceed this, and therefore free them from the earth's gravitational pull? If, as our Lord said, faith can remove a mountain, it can surely take a man to Heaven." [2]

Do you at this very moment possess the faith to know that if the trumpet sounded in the next moment, Christ would catch you up to heaven?

2. Ibid., p. 37.

2 | When Will the Church Be Taken Away?

The prophets, looking down the corridor of history, through the keen eye of the Spirit, usually saw the events associated with the Second Coming so closely related as to be clustered together as one glorious "day of the Lord." Since the Rapture of the Church is but a short prelude to the final consummation of the ages, it sometimes was not seen as a separate event. However, when the partial visions of all the prophets are fitted together and brought into sharp focus by the words of Jesus and His Apostles, we are presented with a clear image that beautifully describes the Rapture as the first in a series of climactic events involving the return of our King. By combining the details given in the Old and New Testaments, we can see the sequence of events shown in the chart on the following page.

BEFORE OR AFTER
THE TRIBULATION?

The present Kingdom of God on earth is the Church. By the Church we mean all born-again believers in Christ. These can be divided into two parts: those who have gone on to heaven, but left their bodies on earth; and those who still live in their bodies on earth at the time of the Rapture. Both parts of the Kingdom will be completely transplanted from earth to heaven in one incredibly swift action. That's what we refer to as the Rapture.

Believers who are very sincere (among them many professors of Bible departments and outstanding authors) hold differing viewpoints on whether the Rapture will take place before or after that great Tribulation which is to immediately precede (Matthew 24:29) the Second Coming of Christ to earth.

Because so many take opposing views on this question, there might appear little hope that this study now presented will resolve anything. Why not just adopt and hold to the idea of one's fa-

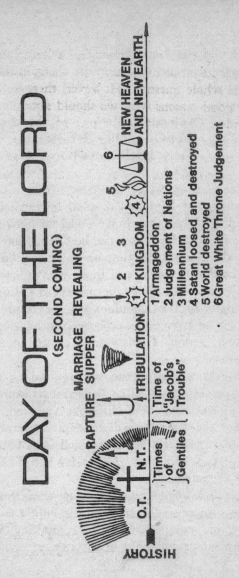

DAY OF THE LORD
(SECOND COMING)

HISTORY

O.T. | N.T.

RAPTURE

MARRIAGE SUPPER

REVEALING

TRIBULATION

Times of Gentiles

Time of "Jacob's Trouble"

KINGDOM

NEW HEAVEN AND NEW EARTH

1 Armageddon
2 Judgement of Nations
3 Millennium
4 Satan loosed and destroyed
5 World destroyed
6 Great White Throne Judgement

vorite professor or author? Or, a more popular attitude might be to merely shift along, indifferent to the whole question. However, there are some very good reasons why we should not take these attitudes. Obviously, only one of the opposing views can be correct, and the other must be incorrect, regardless of the scholarly reputation of its advocates. Christ will either "rapture" the Church before the Tribulation, or He will do so after the Tribulation. Further, any serious misconception of a Bible doctrine affects one's view of the rest of the Bible. No real believer in Christ should be willing to hold to an incorrect understanding of the Word of God. Nor is it any credit to a Christian to be indifferent to any aspect of the Rapture.

WHICH ARE THE TRIBULATION PASSAGES?

Jesus made references to the Tribulation in His Olivet Discourse, recorded in Matthew 24, Mark 13, and Luke 21. Mark's record is essentially the same as Matthew's, but there are some major differences[1] to be found in Matthew 24:15–30 and Luke 21:20–27.

First, the initial signs are different. The abomination of desolation standing in the holy place in Matthew's record differs from the armies sur-

1. Harrison, William K., *Hope Triumphant*, pp. 12–16.

rounding Jerusalem in Luke's record. Second, the two signs introduce two different sets of conditions. Matthew talks of terrible conditions affecting all mankind; Luke tells of what happens to the Jews in particular. Third, in Matthew, great cosmic signs follow the Tribulation and herald the coming of Christ. In Luke, on the other hand, "the times of the Gentiles" immediately follow the capture of Jerusalem. This is that period of history marked by the Gentile domination of Jerusalem, fulfilled between the conquest by the Romans in 70 A.D. and the rebirth of the nation Israel in 1948 A.D. In Luke, the dispersion of the Jews and the times of the Gentiles is followed by the great signs in the heavens.

So we know from history that Luke was first describing the capture of Jerusalem by the Romans and answering the question, "When shall these things be?" (Luke 21:7) before going on to discuss the Great Tribulation. And that question, in its context, clearly refers to the judgment of the Jews and the destruction of the temple. Matthew, on the other hand, gives Jesus' answer to the second question the disciples had asked: "What shall be the sign of thy coming, and of the end of the world [age]?" (Matthew 24:3). The Tribulation is correctly associated with the signs of the end of the age, and the glorious Revelation of Christ.

THE GENERATION

We are aware of certain verses that might be thought to imply that Christ was describing primarily the events of 70 A.D. Did He not say, "This generation shall not pass away, till all be fulfilled?" (Luke 21:32; Matthew 24:34; Mark 13:30). Scholars who believe the generation referred to is that generation living at the time of Christ think the things said in these passages refer to the destruction of Jerusalem in 70 A.D. However, "this generation" could just as easily mean the generation that will see the signs when they *do* appear. If these passages refer only to the destruction of Jerusalem, what shall we do with the very plain statement, ". . . *then* shall appear the sign of the Son of man in heaven: and *then* shall all the tribes of the earth mourn, and they shall see the Son of man coming in the clouds of heaven with power and great glory" (Matthew 24:30)?

In the historical event of A.D. 70, no sign of the Son of man appeared in heaven; not all the tribes of the earth mourned; and no one saw Him on the clouds. Besides, Luke 21:28–32 definitely shows that the term "this generation" refers to one which *at some future time* would see the signs. When the signs were seen, they would indicate that our redemption and the Kingdom of God were near.

In whatever sense the Kingdom of God was not yet present when Jesus spoke these words on this occasion, it is still not present today. Jesus was obviously talking about a form of the Kingdom which none of us have seen. This will appear after the Tribulation, and after the great celestial signs.

THE CHURCH ALREADY CAUGHT AWAY

The Rapture, however, would have already transpired before the events discussed in Matthew 24. Let us look at Revelation 1:19. Christ Himself gives John the outline of the book of Revelation, telling him to write: (1) "The things which thou hast seen" (this vision of Christ); (2) "And the things which are" (characteristics of and warnings to the churches of this age); (3) "And the things which shall be hereafter" (after the Church age).

In John's vision, the seven churches of Asia represented all churches of this age, from the time that Christ established the Church until He returns to catch away His Church (1 Thessalonians 4:13–18). The phrase, "the things which are," described in chapters 2 and 3 of Revelation, is our present Church age. The phrase, "the things which shall be hereafter" applies to chapters 4 through 22, which describe what happens on earth after the Church is taken to heaven. In the original Greek text, the word "hereafter" was "meta tauta," and meant "after these things"—that is, after these things pertaining to the churches. So, when we come to Revelation 4, we are being told that we will now be shown what *God will do* after the Church is gone. Then follows the description of God's dealing with the world during the Tribulation period.

In chapters 4 through 22 of Revelation, the Church has already been caught away to heaven. Here are the proofs:[2]

(1) According to the outline given in Revelation 1:19, this third main division follows the period of the Churches and is a distinct division.

(2) 1 Thessalonians 4:13–18 tells how Christ will catch away the Church, but makes no mention of unbelievers. At that time, He will come to the atmosphere only, and we will "meet the Lord in the air." Later, according to Revelation 19 and Zechariah 14, He will come to the earth itself and stand upon the Mount of Olives, slay the wicked, and set up His Kingdom.

(3) Christ promised the church at Philadelphia (Revelation 3:10) that He would spare her the Tribulation. All of us who are in His Church may now rest on that same promise. (Also, see 1 Thessalonians 1:10; 5:9).

2. Turner, Gwin T., *The Shape of Things to Come*, pp. 17–18.

(4) The best proof is that in chapters 4 to 19, the Church is not mentioned at all—it has disappeared from the earth. In chapter 19:7, 8, 14, the Church reappears, the saints coming with Jesus from heaven. They could not come from heaven if they were not already there.

SIGNS TO LOOK FOR

In point of time, the next event scheduled on the prophetic calendar is the Rapture. How close are we? Very close. God knows the exact hour. He has been gracious in giving us certain signs to look for, so that day would not catch us unprepared. Here are some of them:

1. Israel in her own land again (Zechariah 12:9, 10).
2. Nations from the uttermost north and Arab nations allied against Israel (Daniel 11:40; Ezekiel 38, 39).
3. A ten-nation confederacy out of the descendants of the Roman Empire (Revelation 12:3; 13:1; Daniel 9:26).
4. An army of 200 million on the east (Revelation 9:13–16).
5. A world-wide revival of the mystery religion of Babylon: worship of astrology (Revelation 17:5; Isaiah 47).

6. A great falling away from the true faith by the world's churches (2 Timothy 3:1-5; 2 Thessalonians 2:3).

7. Much scoffing about the doctrine of the Second Coming among unbelievers (2 Peter 3:3, 4).

8. A great outpouring of the Holy Spirit on true Believers—including youth (Joel 2:28).

9. Increase of world travel and technology (Daniel 12:4).

10. Tremendous rise of "cults" and false prophets (Matthew 24:11).

11. Hebrew language revived after being long dead (Zephaniah 3:9).

12. Intensification of war (Matthew 24:6).

13. Outbreak of natural disasters (Matthew 27:7, 8).

14. Increase of pestilences (Matthew 24:7).

15. Heart failure a common cause of death (Luke 21:26).

16. The Gospel preached in all nations (Matthew 24:14).

17. Wastes of Palestine cultivated after many centuries of barrenness (Isaiah 43:19, 20; Ezekiel 34:26, 27; 36:4–10, 30, 34, 35).

18. Hellish war devices (Joel 2:3–5).

When is the Rapture going to occur? Soon. In an instant, in the twinkling of an eye (1 Corinthians 15:52)! When we hear the trumpet, when we see Jesus, when we are transformed into a body of light and join the resurrected saints in the air— it will be quicker than the batting of an eyelash. Be ready! When you are caught up—what activity will you have been busy about? Was it for self, or Savior?

3 | How Do the Rapture and the Second Coming Differ in the Scriptures?

Even beginning Bible students are quick to note that there are some vast differences in some of the passages which describe events involving the return of our Lord. There is a very obvious explanation: there will be two phases of His return, and they are to be different in manner and circumstance! One of the most important passages dealing with the Second Coming is that found in Matthew 24.

THE OLIVET DISCOURSE

The book of Matthew has three important discourses, or sermons. Chapters 5, 6, and 7 contain the famous Sermon on the Mount. Chapter 13 relates an important series of descriptive Parables of the Kingdom. Chapters 24 and 25 contain the Olivet Discourse, so called because of the location where it was given. All three of these discourses have to do with the earthly Kingdom of Christ. The Sermon on the Mount is often called the Constitution of the Kingdom. The Parables of the Kingdom describe various phases the Kingdom will go through, from its inception until the angels gather out of the Kingdom everything that defiles it. The Olivet Discourse deals with a very short period of history: the Tribulation.

The question asked by the disciples in Matthew 24:3 was prompted by their concern for their own nation. The Lord had just said concerning the temple, "There shall not be left here one stone upon another that shall not be thrown down." Also, just moments before, He had said that the nation Israel would not see Him until they would say, "Blessed is he that cometh in the name of the Lord" (Matthew 23:39).

So, it is to that Coming that the disciples naturally refer when they ask, "What shall be the sign of thy coming and of the end of the world [age]?" (Matthew 24:3). That question does not refer to His coming for the Church described in John 14:3. The Church had not yet been formed.[1] Not until

1. Armstrong, Carl, *Signs of Christ's Coming as Son of Man*, p. 11.

32

the Holy Spirit came at Pentecost and baptized believers into one body did the New Testament Church come into being as "the body of Christ." So it was not the coming of the Lord for His Church about which the disciples were concerned at this time. What they had just heard from the Lord's lips would only cause them to think of their own people, their own land, and their temple. In keeping with this, note that when the Lord answers their question, He begins with that with which they, as Jews, would be especially familiar: Many would come to them in His name saying, "I am Christ," (or, I am Messiah), and deceive many (Matthew 24:4–5). One can hardly believe that a true Christian would be deceived by anybody making such a claim. But a Jew, waiting for the Messiah, might very well be deceived by such a false Christ.[2]

The Lord now goes on to speak of that which will affect the whole world at that time. "Ye shall hear of wars and rumors of wars," He says. Some think verse 7 is merely an amplification of the preceding statement. But the increasing racial tension around the globe may well be referred to in "nation rising against nation." Also, "kingdom against kingdom" could apply to the clash of political ideologies that threaten world peace at this very moment. It may be also that famines, pestilences, and earthquakes have already begun the count-

2. Ibid., p. 12.

33

down to the "time of the end." Commenting on these, the Lord says, "All these are the beginning of sorrows" (or, "travail pains," as if nature were pressing on to the birth of a new and better time, and could not rest content or quiet with present evil!).

Then the Lord turns to that which has to do primarily with His ancient people—of whom His disciples are representatives. Matthew 24:9 states, "Then shall they deliver you up to be afflicted." The Lord is referring here to Daniel's "time of great trouble." How the Jews will be delivered up to tribulation is not told here, but passages in the Old Testament do shed light on this. Read Daniel 9:26, 27. A prince shall come who will confirm a covenant with many—that is, with the masses of the Jewish people—for one week. That "one week" is the last of the "seventy weeks" of Daniel's prophecy. It refers to a "seven" of years.

Then read Isaiah 28:14–22. The Jews will make a covenant with hell and death. They would not knowingly make such a covenant, yet this is the way God sees the nature of those with whom the Jews make this covenant, and in whom they place their confidence. Little do they realize that they are delivering themselves to the Tribulation when they sign that covenant.

At the same time, they will be delivering their godly brethren, "the remnant," to the persecution of the antichrist. No doubt the remnant will oppose such a covenant; they will not accept the reign of the antichrist, because they will be looking for another, the true Messiah (Isaiah 25:9). For His name's sake, they will come to be hated by all, not simply because they are Jews, but because of their loyalty to Him whom the world will not receive.[3] And since this hatred will come from "all nations," it will be universal. Such a thing could not take place with the New Testament Church still on earth. The true Church today is still the Jew's best friend. No true Christian could ever hate the Jew because of the Messianic hope, or because of his loyalty to the Messiah.[4] Indeed, it will be the removal of the Church that will make possible the revelation of that wicked one "whom the Lord shall consume with the spirit of His mouth, and shall destroy with the brightness of His coming." The faithful Jews will then be hated not only by the Gentiles, but also by their apostate brethren.

At the same time, many false prophets shall arise and deceive many. It will be a time of lawlessness and violence. The love of many shall wax cold. In direct connection with such a time the Lord says, "But he that shall endure unto the end, the same shall be saved." [5] The Lord spoke these same words

3. Ibid., p. 15.
4. Ibid., p. 15.
5. Ibid., p. 16.

when He commissioned the twelve to preach the Gospel of the Kingdom (Matthew 10:5–22). That is the same Gospel that is referred to here. Those who preach it will be subject to much bitter persecution. Their endurance in and through it all will be a proof of the reality of their faith. The remnant will preach the Gospel of the Kingdom in all the world for a witness unto all nations, and then "shall the end come."

The word that is translated "end" in Matthew 24:3 is different from the word translated "end" in verses 6, 13, and 14. In verse 3, it is properly rendered "consummation" in the best translations. In order to distinguish it from the word used in verses 6, 13, and 14, the word in these verses may be translated as "conclusion." Verse 3 refers to the "consummation of the age," or the last of Daniel's "seventy weeks" of years that covered all prophecy concerning the Jews. Verse 14 refers to the termination of that seven-year period.

At that time, there will be the placing of the "abomination of desolation" in the holy place. The very mention of the holy place implies that there will be a religious center, recognized by the Jews as such. To apply this to any place of Christian worship in this present time is to ignore the plain teaching of the New Testament concerning the Church. According to New Testament Scriptures, the true Church has no particular place on earth which is called *the* holy place as distinguished from all *other* holy places. But the nation Israel *did* have such a place in the tabernacle, and later, the temple.[6] And they will again. The Lord's reference to Daniel's prophecy here should settle it once and for all that He was speaking of the holy place with reference to Daniel's people and his holy city (See Daniel 9:24).

There are two references in the book of Daniel to the "abomination that maketh desolate" (11:31; 12:11). The word translated "abomination" in both places is also used in 1 Kings 11:5, 7 and 2 Kings 23:13 with reference to idols. The term, as used in Daniel, must also refer to an idol. Matthew 24:15 does not tell who it is that will set up this abomination or idol, but Daniel 7:25 tells of a person who will be very prominent in the time of the end. He is the same one as in Revelation 13:1–8, known as "the first beast." There is also another beast mentioned in that same passage (Revelation 13:11–17), known as the "second beast," who will say to them who dwell on the earth that "they should make an image to the beast, which had the wound by a sword, and did live." This second beast has the power to give life or breath "to the image of the beast, that the image of the beast should both speak, and cause that as many as would not worship the image of the beast should be killed" (Revelation 13:15). It is reasonable to suppose that this image will be set up in the holy place, because the placing of an image in any other holy place would have little or no sig-

6. Ibid., p. 20.

nificance to the Jew. But the setting up of any kind of image in the temple is expressly forbidden in Jewish law (Exodus 20:4–6). Such a procedure would be utterly shocking to a God-fearing Jew and would well serve as a signal for the flight that our Lord suggested in Matthew 24:16.[7]

All of this assumes the existence of a place which the Jews will recognize as their *holy place*. Possibly the dictator or prince of the New Roman Empire will provide for this in his covenant with Israel. "Then let them which be in Judea flee into the mountains" (Matthew 24:16). Note that the Lord does not refer to any other location in the world—not even to Rome. Attention in that day will be focused upon Jerusalem and Judea.[8] It was said to Daniel, "Seventy weeks are determined upon thy people and upon thy holy city" (Daniel 9:24).

Several times in recent years, I have noticed that it is still the custom in Israel for men to spend time on the housetop. But the news of the setting up of an idol in the holy place might reach some even while at work in the field. Neither the one taking his leisure on the housetop nor the one busy in the field will have time to stop for anything when the news breaks. They will have to flee immediately in order to escape the consequences of refusing to worship the image. Note the Lord's expressed pity

7. Ibid., p. 22.
8. Ibid., p. 23.

for those who are with child and those that give suck in those days. The implication is that no consideration will be shown them because of their delicate condition, nor because they have the care of helpless babies. History will repeat itself and "they shall fall by the sword," their infants shall be dashed in pieces, and their women with child shall be ripped up (Hosea 13:16). Usually such barbaric atrocities are associated with ancient history. However, current history shows that "man's inhumanity to man" still knows no limits. "Then shall be great tribulation, such as was not since the beginning of the world to this time, no, nor ever shall be" (Matthew 24:21). It will be so awful that it will threaten the existence of the whole human race. "Except those days should be shortened, there should no flesh be saved" (Matthew 24:22). During that time the faithful Jews will turn to Christ. It must not be thought that because the Holy Spirit will have completed His work of forming and calling out the Church that He will then have nothing further to do on earth. The Lord will pour His Spirit upon His ancient people Israel so that when they look upon Him whom they pierced, they will recognize Him and mourn because of Him (Zechariah 12:10). And that same blessed Spirit will be their protection then, no matter how clever may be the enemy's attempt to deceive.

At the close of this period, the greatest blackout in history will occur. "Immediately after the tribulation of those days shall the sun be darkened, and the moon shall not give her light, and the stars shall fall from heaven . . ." (Matthew 24:29). "And then shall appear the sign of the Son of man in heaven; and then shall all the tribes of the earth mourn" (Matthew 24:30), just as Zechariah also predicted long ago. The mention of "tribes" suggests that this is special reference to that people which is so well known for its tribal divisions. The reason for their mourning is not given in Matthew 24, but in Zechariah 12:10 we are told that they will be recognizing the One whom they had previously rejected and pierced.

One highly significant fact that points out that this is not His Coming for the Church is revealed in Matthew 24:31. ". . . he shall send his angels . . . and they shall gather his elect from the four winds, from one end of heaven to the other." When Jesus comes for His Church, he will not make use of such agencies to gather His own to Himself. 1 Thessalonians 4:16 plainly says that "the Lord himself shall descend from heaven" to summon His own to meet Him "in the air." In Matthew 24:31, there is not even a hint that He will remove His elect from the earth to heaven. It should also be noted here that there is no reference to the Resurrection of the dead, whereas the Resurrection of the dead in Christ is one of the outstanding features of the Lord's Coming for His Church. As a matter of fact, there is no reference to the Resurrection of the dead anywhere in the Olivet Discourse. A matter so important would certainly have been included there if that discussion had to do with the Rapture. It can be concluded that Matthew 24 does not refer to the Rapture of the New Testament Church, as some think. It refers to the time of the Tribulation, which ends in a Second Coming of Christ that is quite different from the Rapture.

NEW TESTAMENT RAPTURE PASSAGES

The primary thoughts usually associated with the Rapture are concisely given in the passage in 1 Thessalonians 4:14–17. There, Jesus comes only to the earth's atmosphere, and according to the parallel passage in John 14:1–3, He then takes the believers to heaven to be with Him there. The resurrection referred to in 1 Thessalonians 4 and the simultaneous transformation of living bodies into immortal bodies described in 1 Corinthians 15 are not at all mentioned in the Matthew 24 or in the Zechariah 14 passages. The reason is that these last two passages refer to the glorious and triumphant Second Coming of the Lord Jesus Christ. In that Coming, Jesus will plant His foot on the Mount of Olives. He will set up a seat of judgment (Matthew 25) and bring about a literal fulfillment of the Old Testament promises to restore the Kingdom of David. After this Coming, the Lord will remain on earth to rule for a thousand years (Revelation 20:4–6). In this latter Coming, He will be seen by all on the earth at that time (Revelation 1:7). In the Rapture, He obviously will be seen only by those for whom He comes, since this takes place in the twinkling of an eye (1 Corinthians 15:52).

THE SEQUENCE IN JOHN'S REVELATION

The Rapture is not specifically mentioned in the book of Revelation. The letters to the churches (Revelation 2 and 3) can be taken as a narrative of the New Testament Church through its entire life up to the point of the Rapture. If a mention of the Rapture is to be found in the book of Revelation, it should be seen in the very next chapter; and that is just where we discover it. Revelation 4:1, 2 reads, "After these things I looked, and behold, a door standing open in heaven, and the first voice which I heard, like the sound of a trumpet speaking with me, said, Come up here, and I will show you. . . ." And then John goes on to say, "Immediately I was in the spirit, and behold, a throne was standing in heaven, and one sitting on the throne."

This passage is the only one in the book of Revelation which by its language resembles the description of the Rapture given in 1 Thessalonians 4:16, 17 and in 1 Corinthians 15:51, 52. Note: more than one voice is indicated by the words "first voice." It is like the sound of a trumpet. John is caught up to heaven, to the presence of the Lord. The action is immediate, and it takes place right after the Church age. If the Rapture is mentioned in the book of Revelation, this must be it. Of course, this mention is not the Rapture itself—it is merely a symbolic representation based on John's experience nineteen centuries ago. In the light of this study in its entirety, this mention is found exactly where we would expect to find it.[9]

Now read Revelation 4:4; 5:9, 10. These verses refer to the twenty-four elders. In the Bible, the term "elder" is used only of men, never of angels. These men are in heaven, close to the throne of God. Only redeemed men are in heaven. These men not only wear the white garments of purity and righteousness (Revelation 4:4), but they are enthroned and wearing golden crowns, the symbol of victory and authority. They praise the Lord because He has redeemed men of every nation and tribe, who shall reign on the earth at some future time. Here in this passage, at a time

9. Harrison, William K., *Hope Triumphant*, p. 77.

prior to the Tribulation, we see redeemed and glorified men who already possess their crowns—their rewards. Such rewards are to be given at the Coming of the Lord for the Church (2 Timothy 4:8), when the Lord will judge the stewardship of His people (2 Corinthians 5:10; 1 Corinthians 3:10–15). This passage then must mean that the saints are represented as elders.[10] The term "elder" is used many times in the Bible to signify the rulers or representatives of the people. Most scholars agree that the twenty-four elders symbolically represent the whole Church; the twelve tribes of Israel and the twelve New Testament Apostles. Keep in mind as you read the following chapters of Revelation that the Church has already been raptured, or caught up to heaven.

But in Revelation 19, we find something different. The Coming of Jesus mentioned there has to do with that same Coming referred to in Matthew 25:31, Zechariah 14:3 and 2 Thessalonians 1:7, 8. Prior to that event and the Tribulation period it will close, the Church will have been caught away in a silent, sudden Coming of the Lord Jesus Christ. The two Comings are distinctly described in a single passage of Scripture in Isaiah 26:19–21. In verse 19 is a description of the Resurrection at the time of the Rapture. In verse 20, we have the Church safely in heaven during the Tribulation, and in verse 21, the Second Coming.

10. Ibid., p. 78.

As sure as God is true, both descriptions of His Coming will be literally fulfilled: the Rapture of the Church, and the victorious conquest of earth. Both events hold unimaginable adventure for us who wait for Christ.

Caught up! Caught up! No wing required!
Caught up to Him, by love inspired,
To meet Him in the air!
Spurning the earth with upward bound,
Not casting a single glance around,
Nor listing a single earth-born sound,
Caught up in the radiant air!
Caught up with rapture and surprise!
Caught up! Our fond affections rise
Our coming Lord to meet!
Hearing the trumpet's glorious sound,
Soaring to join the rising crowd,
Gazing beyond the parted cloud,
Beneath His pierc-ed feet! *

from *God's Prophecies for Plain People*
by William L. Pettingill

* Permission by Van Kampen Press, Wheaton, Illinois

4 | What Will Happen to Those Caught Away in the Rapture?

WHERE WILL WE GO?

Where is the "third heaven" (2 Corinthians 12:2) that the Apostle Paul called "Paradise" (2 Corinthians 12:4)? Plainly, it is where the dying thief went the day he said to Jesus, "Lord, remember me when thou comest into thy kingdom" (Luke 23:42). Jesus said that is where He Himself would be, as well as the thief. He told His disciples that He was going there to prepare a place for them (John 14:2, 3) and that He would come again to take them there to be with Him. In 1 Thessalonians 4:17, we are assured that from the moment of the Rapture, we will never again be separated from Jesus: ". . . and so shall we ever be with the Lord."

Where is God the Father's dwelling place located (1 Kings 8:30; Daniel 2:28; Matthew 5:45; Hebrews 8:1)? His dwelling place is that same "Paradise" mentioned by Jesus and Paul. It is where the throne of God is (Isaiah 6:1; Ezekiel 1:26–28; Revelation 4:2–5). It is a place not limited by concepts of time—a zone that presently exists as "eternity" (Isaiah 57:15). Genesis 1:14–18 plainly tells us that God's purpose in creating all the stars, the sun, and the moon, was to set up a cosmic timepiece. Our knowledge of "time" is the result of God putting the known universe together in such a way that "lights in the heavens" are for "seasons, and for days and years" (Genesis 1:14). The heaven where God dwells knows no such limitations. It is therefore completely removed from known space. That is where the raptured Church will be the next instant after the trumpet sounds! It is a real, physical environment. If it were not, what need would we have for bodies? In God's heaven, there are real mansions (many of them), according to our Lord's own Word in John 14:2.

WHAT WILL WE SEE?

In the house of God in heaven, a great victory banquet and marriage supper is being prepared (Matthew 22:2-4; Revelation 19:7-9). We all are being invited, but only those who are properly dressed in the wedding garment of the righteousness of Christ will be permitted to attend (Matthew 22:11-13; Revelation 19:8). Imagine the dazzling beauty of the setting in which this most spectacular of all celebrations will take place! If a solitary rainbow can cause one to catch his breath in admiration, what will it be like when thousands of them drape the walls of that banquet hall? If a floor of finely polished Italian marble is a thing of beauty here, what will that shining sea of crystal-clear glass be under our feet there?

And think of our appearance in the likeness of the shining Christ of Revelation 1, the dazzling Christ of the Transfiguration, the brilliant Lord met by Paul on the Damascus road! (Revelation 1:15, 16; Matthew 17:2; Acts 26:13-15). The prophet Daniel foresaw that the redeemed would have the appearance of bright stars (Daniel 12:3). And, even if it were possible to find monotony in seeing a sameness in all these shining bodies, we are told in 1 Corinthians 15:41, 42 that there will be distinct and different glories given to our Resurrection bodies. Jesus says we will shine forth like the sun (Matthew 13:43). We cannot fully comprehend what effect this experience of such a transformed appearance will have on us, but we do know that we will be immensely pleased (1 John 3:2; 1 Corinthians 2:9; Psalms 17:15).

The first moment after the Rapture will be spent in breathless gazing upon our Lord, whom we shall see face to face. Rewards will be given out during that victory jubilee, but what reward can compare with just seeing the King of Kings! When a president or some other head of state arrives in a city for a ceremony or parade, thousands of eager citizens press against each other for just a look at this great and famous person. But what is the mere sight of an earthly dignitary compared with beholding Jesus!

And then, the hills of heaven will echo with glad shouts and hallelujahs (Revelation 19:6)! John gives us an idea of what will take place: "I heard a great voice of much people in heaven saying, Alleluia; Salvation, and glory, and honor, and power, unto the Lord our God" (Revelation 19:1). What a wonderful time of reunion will take place there! Mothers and fathers lost years ago in death will be found again by their once-heartbroken children! Long separated Christian friends will embrace each other again when death has been swallowed up in victory! Someone once asked D. L. Moody if he thought we would recognize one another in heaven. "Certainly," he said, "we are surely not going to be less intelligent there than we are here!" God's Word affirms in 1 Corinthians 13:12 that we shall know as we are also known.

What about children in heaven? They will be known and recognized, but their earthly bodies, which were immature, will have flowered into the perfection of a Resurrection body like our own. Oh, the happy surprises that await so many families!

There will, of course, be a significant change in our inter-personal relationships. While we will in no wise be deprived of our happiness in being re-united with loved ones and friends, we will truly all be children of God, and therefore every one of us will be sisters and brothers in the same family (Luke 20:36). Our Lord Jesus explained that no problem would arise in cases where on earth widows had remarried after the death of a husband (Luke 20:35). They will simply be happy children of God together. Our Resurrection bodies will be far superior to our present bodies, and since there will be no death in heaven, there will be no necessity for procreation; reproductive organs and sex drives will be obsolete. Marriage will no longer be necessary (Luke 20:35). As to the physical and emotional happiness derived now from these things in our present state, we will discover that things far superior have been prepared for our continual pleasure (1 Corinthians 2:9).

WHAT WILL WE DO?

After we have taken brief note of our new surroundings, gazed upon the Lord Jesus Christ, enjoyed reunion with our loved-ones, and taken account of our new bodies, we will then move to the banquet room of heaven and sit before the table Jesus has been preparing for the Church, His Holy Bride (Revelation 19:7; Ephesians 5:25–27; Matthew 25:10). What a gathering that will be! (See the description in Hebrews 12:22–24.)

Then, immediately following, we will move to the great throne room of heaven (Revelation 4: 2–5) or stand before the Seat of Christ there in the same location as the marriage supper. At that time, each saint will give an account of himself before the Judgment Seat of Christ (Romans 14:10, 12; Matthew 12:36; Hebrews 13:17). This will be our time of accounting for the words we have said, the places of service we have been given on earth (Matthew 19:28–30; 20:1–16; Luke 13:6; 1 Corinthians 3:12–15). What will be the basis of rewards given at that time? Matthew 6:1–6 and 10:39–42 record for us the very words of Jesus on that subject, and therefore ought to be carefully studied. In 2 Corinthians 5:10 and 1 Corinthians 4:5, we are told definitely that every one of us who stands before the Judgment Seat of Christ will receive exactly what we have worked to accomplish on earth. (Note "receive the things done," and compare this with Matthew 6:19, 20.) Very evidently, our earthly service to the Lord Jesus Christ has a direct bearing on what we will receive at that time. We are also reminded in 2 John 8 that there is a danger of backsliding and losing rewards we had earlier accumulated (1 Corinthians 3:13–15; 2 Corinthians 5:10). These passages make us consider what deposits and withdrawals have been made lately in our treasure-account in heaven. John, in the verse mentioned above, urges us to see to it that we get a "full reward," and not let Satan cheat us out of what is already ours. Revelation 3:11 tells us that Jesus said that He is coming quickly (unexpectedly) and tells us to "hold fast" that which we have, lest someone else get the crown of reward meant for us! There is no doubt about it; "steadfastness," "faithfulness," "continuing," and similar words are mentioned often in God's Word for a reason!

At the marriage supper and Judgment Seat of Christ, it will not matter so much what we did for Christ when we first started out; the important thing will be what we *continued to do!* And let us remember this: it is not works done in the energy of the flesh we will be rewarded for, but works done by the Spirit through us (Romans 8:1, 9; Philippians 1:21; Galatians 2:16, 20). If we study carefully the above Scriptures, we will understand why it is so very important to let the

Spirit of Christ completely possess us and work in us (Romans 12:1; John 14:12–14). He really is a living Lord, and lives in His believers! Great will be the reward of those who have let Him manifest His Spirit continually through their lives!

HOW LONG WILL WE BE CAUGHT AWAY

After the great rejoicing of that Banquet and receiving of those rewards, it will soon be time to return to earth at the close of the seven-year period between the Rapture and the Second Coming. We are promised the privilege of returning and reigning with Him, before whom every knee will then bow and confess that He is Christ and Lord (1 Corinthians 6:2; Revelation 19:14; Luke 19:17–19; Revelation 20:4, 6).

When we reappear on earth, we will appear with immortal bodies, accompanied by millions of mighty angels, and led by the King of Kings! What a glorious thought! (Revelation 19:11–14; Matthew 24:30, 31; 25:31; Revelation 5:9, 10).

My friend, you need to carefully consider these matters. In the moment of that Second Coming, you may be among those who stand with the Lord and see the judgment and destruction of every last unbeliever on earth—or, if you have rejected Jesus

Christ, you may be one of those who has by then been deceived by the antichrist and will share the fate of those who, in Matthew 25:46, go away into everlasting punishment! Which would it be—if the Rapture of all believers took place this very second? Hurry, friend! Hurry to Christ now!

5 | What Will Happen to Unbelievers During the Rapture?

Nothing! In a split-second all that takes place in the Rapture of believers will be completely over (1 Corinthians 15:52). The unbelievers will have had absolutely no warning, no awareness of what was taking place; but suddenly, it will have happened! When they know about it, it will be too late! (Matthew 24:38, 39, 50, 51).

There will be two kinds of unbelievers when the Rapture occurs: living and dead. Neither group will hear the sound of the trumpet, the shout of the Lord, or the voice of the archangel (1 Thessalonians 4:16). Not one individual unbeliever will be "caught up" by mistake. There are no such errors made in the books kept in heaven.

WHAT ABOUT THE UNSAVED DEAD?

The dead "out of Christ" will remain in their graves, awaiting the final Resurrection in the Great White Throne Judgment at the end of the Kingdom Period of earth's history (Revelation 20:5, 11–15). Actually, the "person," or "soul" of the unbeliever will already be in hell, and will remain there until "death and hell" give up the dead which are in them at the end of time (Luke 16:22, 23; Revelation 20:13). Only the physical body, buried at the time of physical death, goes to the grave. These organic remains have no feelings or sense of time (Ecclesiastes 3:20, 21), but there is no interruption of consciousness for the person who passes through the experience of physical death. This is true whether the person is saved (2 Corinthians 5:8), or lost (Luke 16:23), since the soul is an eternal spirit (Ecclesiastes 8:8; Genesis 2:7; 1 Thessalonians 5:23; Psalms 31:15). Since the lost souls in hell cannot be raptured as part of the Church, they must remain there to await the last Judgment where much more terrible punishment will be meted out (Revelation 20:12, 13).

WHAT WILL LIVING
UNBELIEVERS DO?

The living unbeliever will be shocked and dazed as he suddenly discovers that the prophecies of the Rapture have been realized. Indeed, the world will go into a panic of planet-wide proportions! Imagine the headlines of the newspapers the morning after the Rapture:

"Thousands of Missing Persons Reports Filed"
"Mysterious Disappearances Worldwide"
"President Declares State of Emergency"
"Industries Paralyzed: Workers Gone"
"59 Planes Crash; Pilots Still Missing"
"Transatlantic Cable Jammed with
Distress Messages"
"U.N. Called into Emergency Session"
"Major Highways Jammed by Abandoned
Cars"
"Masses Crowd into Churches Around World"
"Mothers Cry for Missing Babies"
"Millions of Graves Found Open and Empty"

Yes, there will be many "missing persons" immediately after that blessed moment, but there will be others who are left (Luke 17:34–36). How many? There will be a far greater number in this category than any of us have imagined. There is not a city or a county or a state, to my knowledge, where the devil does not have more children than the Lord (John 8:44). In fact, I know of no place in the world where the devil does not have a majority of the people under his control. He is the "prince of this world" for the time being (Ephesians 2:2, 3; 6:12; John 12:31).

Nowhere in the Scriptures is it claimed that the whole world shall be brought to the feet of Christ in this dispensation. In the fifteenth chapter of Acts, James says, "Simeon hath declared how God at the first did visit the Gentiles, *to take out of them* a people for his name" (Acts 15:14). It is God's plan that we, the Gentile nations, be given a dispensation of time during which a great number of people will turn from the world to Him (Luke 21:24; Romans 11:25). But He is saving a people out of the wreckage of the world (Ephesians 2:12, 13; 3:5, 6; Colossians 1:12, 13). Many are being called (2 Peter 3:9; Matthew 9:13), but few are finding the way (Matthew 7:14; Luke 12:51–53; 1 John 5:19). The greatest part of the world population will be left behind at the time of the Rapture (2 Peter 2:9). That is why it is not safe to "go along with the crowd." We are told to separate ourselves from the world's ways (2 Corinthians 6:17; James 4:4; 1 Peter 2:9–11), and be different (Titus 2:14; 2 Corinthians 5:17). It is important to be different on the inside as well as be different on the outside (Matthew 23:25, 26;

Romans 8:9; Ephesians 5:18, 19; Galatians 5:22; John 3:7).

During the Rapture, those who have not the Spirit of Christ, because they were not born again in this spiritual way, will be left behind for a very obvious reason. Though the Lord will return as a "thief in the night," He is not coming to steal. "If any man have not the Spirit of Christ, he is none of his" (Romans 8:9). Jesus will catch up only those who have been bought by His blood and belong to Him (1 Corinthians 6:19, 20).

BELIEVERS WILL BE PREPARED

Thank God! I am a child of the King by spiritual adoption (Romans 8:14–16). I have been made a part of the family of God. To us in the family of God is the blessed promise made in 1 Thessalonians 5:9, "For God hath not appointed us to wrath, but to obtain salvation by our Lord Jesus Christ." Our Lord does not intend for us to face the Tribulation, which is the time of His wrath on the earth. However, the unbeliever must be given full and fair warning that once he misses this greatest of all appointments—there will be no way in which the damage can be repaired. Jesus says in the last chapter of the blessed Book, "Behold, I come quickly" (Revelation 22:7). "He that is unjust, let him be unjust still; and he which is filthy, let him be filthy still: and he which is righteous, let him be righteous still: and he that is holy, let him be holy still" (Revelation 22:11). Reader, if you are unprepared for the Rapture at this very moment, do not waste away another precious second of the time God is giving you! Listen to the "countdown" in the ticking of the clock. Hear it in your own heartbeat. Heed the "signs" given us in Matthew 24, Mark 13, and Luke 21. They are on the front page of your paper every morning! It is near, "even at the doors." Bow before the invisible King who is at your own heart's door right now. By faith, call out in prayer and beg forgiveness and receive Him as Lord of all your life! "To as many as received him, to them gave he power to become the sons of God" (John 1:12). Believe it! Be ready!

6

After the Rapture, What Will Happen to Unbelievers Left on Earth?

The answer to that question lies in the very purpose of the Rapture:

> "Thy dead men shall live, together with my dead body shall they arise. Awake and sing, ye that dwell in dust: for thy dew is as the dew of herbs, and the earth shall cast out the dead. Come, my people, enter thou into thy chambers, and shut thy doors about thee; hide thyself as it were for a little moment, until the indignation be overpast" (Isaiah 26:19, 20).

God's "dead men" will be raised up in the Resurrection, and God's people living on earth at that time will be gathered into their "chambers" in God's house (John 14:2) to remain there in safety until the "indignation" passes over. Obviously, the purpose of the Rapture is to provide believers with an escape from this "little moment" of earth's history, which is described as the time of "indignation."

GOD'S INDIGNATION

This same word is found in Romans 2:8, 9. In that passage we are told that "indignation and wrath, tribulation and anguish" will come at a specific time called "the day of wrath" (Romans 2:5). The word "indignation" is found also in another passage about the "day of the Lord" in Isaiah 13:4–11. In verse 5, we read:

> "They come from a far country, from the end of heaven, even the Lord, and the weapons of his indignation. . . ."

"His indignation" means here that it is the Lord's own. But we see also that there are specific "weapons" for bringing it upon the earth. We read a detailed description of those weapons in Revelation, chapters 7–10, in the sounding by the angels of seven trumpets, and in Revelation 16, where the seven angels pour out the seven vials of God's wrath upon the earth. The word "indignation" is repeated in a similar passage in Zephaniah 3:8. Other descriptions are found in Zephaniah 1:14, 15, Revelation 7:14, Jeremiah 30:7, and Daniel 12:1. In Jeremiah 30:7, it is called the "time of Jacob's trouble." In Daniel 12:1, it is a "time of trouble," during which Daniel's people, the Jews, would be delivered—if their names were found written in "the book"! Jesus, in Matthew 24:21, calls it a time of "great tribulation." He also indicates that this will be a short period of history (verse 22). In Revelation, chapter 7, we see a great multitude in heaven, saved during the "great tribulation" (verses 9 and 14).

From these and other Scriptures, we conclude that there will ensue, immediately after the Rapture of the Gentile Church, a terrible period of suffering and trouble on earth. It is known as "the Tribulation period" by students of prophecy. It is the time when the world's wickedness will catch up with it, and God's righteous judgments, or punishments, will reveal His indignation at the corruption of His creation (Isaiah 13:11; 26:21; Zephaniah 3:8; Romans 2:6; Romans 8:21, 22; Revelation 11:18). It will come after the "times of the Gentiles" are fulfilled (Luke 21:24) and, according to the chronological order in Luke 21, will be a time of distress and terrible natural catastrophies, concluded by the glorious Second Coming of Jesus (Luke 21:27).

DANIEL'S LAST "WEEK"

This short period of history that begins with the Rapture and ends with the Return, or Second Coming, is generally held to be about seven years in length. In his ninth chapter, Daniel gives a description of all future Jewish history which will be fulfilled in seventy "weeks" of years. After giving details for sixty-nine of the "weeks," Daniel tells us that in the midst of a week of years (or in the middle of a seven-year period) the antichrist will break his seven-year covenant with the Jews and cause the newly reinstated Jewish Temple to cease its program of sacrifice and worship (Daniel 9:27). Revelation 13:5 says he will be given power to continue for forty-two months, exactly three and a half years. Daniel was told in the closing statement of the vision given to him, that from the time the daily sacrifices cease, 1,290 days will be left (Daniel 12:11). This is approximately the same three and a half years, and if we take this as the second half of the "week" mentioned in Daniel 9:27, we conclude that the period is roughly seven years.

Another reference that supports this conclusion

is that made to "a time, times, and the dividing of time," in Daniel 7:25 and 12:7. This also is understood to mean "a year, two years, and a half year," or three and a half years. These last years are more specifically the "time of Jacob's trouble" than the whole seven years. It will be a time when the "power of the holy people" will be scattered (Daniel 12:7). When no hope for them seems to be left, then they shall suddenly be delivered by Christ, and turn to Him for their salvation (Zechariah 12:9, 10; 13:1; 14:2). No doubt, their conversion will be precipitated by the wonderful deliverance in Ezekiel 39 and Zechariah 14, but it will certainly be the result of hearing the gospel preached by 144,000 divinely protected Jewish evangelists (Revelation 7:3, 4; 14:16).

DAY OF ANTICHRIST

The Scriptures teach that the faith of believers during this period will be tested to its utmost limits (Matthew 24:22, 24). We read of the "beast," or antichrist in Revelation 13:7:

> "And it was given unto him to make war with the saints, and to overcome them. . . ."

Evidently, the price of not worshipping the Beast will be immediate execution (Revelation 6:1; 13:15). But there will be some who are willing to receive Christ anyway, "loving not their lives unto the death" (Revelation 12:11). These will be those "saved out of great tribulation" (Revelation 7:14).

TIME OF SUFFERING

This is the time when Israel will pass through the refiner's fire (Zechariah 13:9) and only one third will come through. This is the time when peace will be taken from the earth (Revelation 6:4). During this time, one fourth of the people will die in war, famine, disease, etc. (Revelation 6:8); and then one third of those that are left will be destroyed in a terrible conquest (perhaps through nuclear warfare) by an army of 200 million moving westward across the Euphrates river (Revelation 9:15, 16). We read of this time:

> "And in those days shall men seek death,
> and shall not find it, and shall desire to
> die, and death shall flee from them"
> (Revelation 9:6).

Imagine that! The people who are not killed in the awful judgments of God's indignation will wish they were! They will even beg the mountains to fall on them (Revelation 6:15-17). But death shall flee from them! People who slash their wrists won't bleed to death. People who jump from tall buildings may be hopelessly crippled, but not killed. People who shoot or stab themselves will be horribly wounded, but will not die. Those who throw themselves in front of cars or trains may be hideously mangled, but not released from their suffering by anything so merciful as death. What a terrifying time!

This is what is reserved for the unbeliever who is not prepared for the Rapture (2 Peter 2:9, and Romans 2:8, 9): (1) At first, bewilderment and numbness upon discovery that the Rapture is real and has already taken place! Then (2), a false sense of hope as the "prince" takes over and sets up a world government. (3) After three and a half years, terrible (*unbelievably* terrible) suffering and destruction for another three and a half years.

ESCAPE?

The purpose of the Rapture is to show God's loving care of His children by delivering them from having to live on earth during this Tribulation period. Remember what Jesus said:

"Watch ye therefore, and pray always, that ye may be accounted worthy to escape all these things that shall come to pass, and to stand before the Son of man" (Luke 21:36).

That's where I'm going to be during the Tribulation period: standing up there in heaven where Jesus is! You can be there with us, reader, if you are willing to let Christ be your Lord and Savior! But this chapter is meant to be a sincere and heavy-hearted warning to any lost soul that may have his name on the "church roll," but not in the Book of Life (Revelation 20:15). If you have never really been "born again" (John 3:7), ask yourself the following question: "When the real Christians and the real churches are gone, what will I do?" That moment may be sooner than you think. "Even so, come, Lord Jesus!"

7 | When Will the Resurrection of the Lost Take Place?

The Rapture will be the occasion of mass resurrection of all the dead who are true believers (1 Thessalonians 4:16) and the instantaneous "catching up" of all the living believers (1 Thessalonians 4:17; 1 Corinthians 15:52). But no mention of lost souls being raised is made in any of the passages about the Rapture. Study carefully 1 Thessalonians 4; 1 Corinthians 15; Philippians 3:20, 21; John 14:1–3; Isaiah 26:19, 20; and Revelation 19: 7–9).

Truly, the Lord will come as a "thief in the night" (1 Thessalonians 5:2); but this means that He will come unexpectedly, without warning. It does not mean that He is coming to take what is not His. Romans 8:9 tells us, "If any man have not the Spirit of Christ, he is none of his." These will be left behind.

ANOTHER RESURRECTION

What about these dead "out of Christ," who are not raised and caught away to heaven in the Rapture? When will their bodies be raised?

A key passage for our understanding of this question is Revelation 20:4–6, 11–15. Very clearly, they will not be raised until a period of 1,000 years has expired. It is, especially, "*the* thousand years," denoting a definite chapter of world history yet to come. It is clearly defined as beginning with the return of Christ (or Second Coming) in Revelation 19:11–16, and ending with the temporary loosing and final destruction of Satan in Revelation 20:7–10. At the close of this millenial period (or as we prefer to call it, Kingdom period), the rest of the dead will be raised. They will be raised to appear before the Great White Throne to be judged according to their works (Revelation 20:11–15).

A LONG WAIT IN HELL

Apparently the dead out of Christ, who now languish in hell (Luke 16:22, 23; Revelation 20:13), will await their final judgment and disposition for eternity until God is ready to do away with the present heaven and earth and create a new, eternal earth (Revelation 20:11; 21:1; 2 Peter 3:10–13). At the Rapture, however, they may have already been imprisoned in hell for many years or centuries. But however long it has been since their bodies returned to the dust, they will wait still longer before any change whatsoever. For the Rapture will be followed by a seven-year period of tribulation on earth (see our discussion in the preceding chapter). This will be followed by an undetermined period including the return of Christ, the destruction of the armies of antichrist, the setting up of Christ's seat of government in Jerusalem, the judgment of nations (Matthew 25:32), and the destruction of all living unbelievers (Matthew 25:46; Revelation 19:11, 12). This will probably be a very quick succession of events. Then the thousand years will begin (Revelation 20:4, 6; Daniel 7:9–11, 13–14, 21, 22, 27). It will be an everlasting kingdom, but will be located on this present earth for only a thousand years.

After that, there is the "little season" (Revelation 20:3, 7–10) that Satan is released before his final assignment to the "lake of fire." Then, and only then, the rest of the dead will be raised.

THE RESURRECTION OF DAMNATION

"But," some will ask, "what about other Scriptures which seem to teach a general Resurrection where the lost and saved are raised together?" I am afraid that concept exists in our hymn-book more than in the Bible. It is a problem only where there has been careless reading. For instance, Daniel 12:2 says that some will awake to everlasting life, and some to everlasting contempt. There is nothing here that says this will happen simultaneously—only that the Resurrection of some will have consequences different from that of others. Another example of Scripture that requires careful reading in order to be understood is John 5:28, 29:

> "Marvel not at this: for the hour is coming, in the which all that are in the graves shall hear his voice, And shall come forth, they that have done good, unto the resurrection of life; and they that have done evil, unto the resurrection of damnation."

Again, nothing is said about this being one event. Indeed, it is very significant that two specific resurrections are named in this passage: The Resurrection of life, and the Resurrection of damnation. These are the first and second Resurrections referred to in Revelation 20. In that chapter, it is made very clear that they will be separated by a great period of time.

BY WHAT POWER?

How will the lost dead be raised? They will be raised by the command of God. There is not the slightest doubt in my mind that the God who could assemble this universe by mere vocal commands (Genesis 1) can also re-assemble every element of every cell of a decayed body!

But the resurrected bodies of the lost souls will be no pleasant sight. Their unredeemed natures will cause their appearance to be horrible. No cosmetics will be available then—and the ravages of sin on their bodies will be there for all to see. (Study Romans 3:13, 14; Isaiah 1:5, 6; Romans 1:28–32; Galatians 6:7, 8.) Especially consider this: "He that soweth to his flesh shall of the flesh reap corruption. . . ." (Galatians 6:8). Truly, "Blessed and holy is he that hath part in the first resurrection. . . ." (Revelation 20:6). Read again 1 Thessalonians 4:16, 17. Are you "in Christ"?

The Rapture is the "catching up" of the dead and living who are "in Christ". It can take place any second now. Are you ready?

THE GREAT WHITE THRONE

The immediate purpose of the Resurrection of lost souls is the judgment described in Revelation 20—the Great White Throne Judgment. This will be the final judgment. Every lost soul who has ever lived on earth will appear before God (Revelation 20:12) and receive sentence according to the amount of evil they have done (Revelation 20:12, 13). This will include all who have died in the dispensation of time prior to the Rapture, all who will die during the terrible visitations of God's wrath upon the earth during the Tribulation (Revelation 6:8; 9:18), all those destroyed by Christ at the conclusion of Armageddon (Revelation 19:21), all who are slain in the judgment of nations (Matthew 25:46), and all those who are deceived by Satan during the "little season" when he is loosed after the Millenium (Revelation 20:8, 9).

This judgment is consistent with the righteous nature of God, who is never unequal in His dealings with any soul. When the present keeping-place of the lost dead (hell) gives place to God's new order in Revelation 21:1, and is done away with (Revelation 20:14), God will cause hell to give up its contents before the Great White Throne (Revelation 20:13). There, before final consignment to the "lake of fire," a just determination of the degrees of punishment deserved will be made (Revelation 20:12).

THE LAKE OF FIRE

There is a scriptural distinction between "hell" and the "Lake of Fire," both of which are mentioned in Revelation 20:14. Hell, as pictured in Luke 16, is the place of torment where a lost person is immediately, consciously located upon physical death (Luke 16:22c, 23). It is a place of suffering (verse 24). But while it is an awful fate in itself, it is chiefly a holding place for the lost (verse 26) where every soul suffers more or less equally. However, when hell gives up the dead which are in it, and the sentence of the Great White Throne Judgment is pronounced, the Lake of Fire receives both the container and the contained (Revelation 20:13–15). There, apparently, the eternally damned will experience varying degrees of punishment, "according to their works" (verses 12 and 13). Hell is temporary; the Lake of Fire is eternal (Revelation 14:11).

The dead "out of Christ" can only await this resurrection. Unlike the resurrection joyously anticipated by believers, this one holds no joy, no deliverance, no rest. The two resurrections are as different as heaven and hell. Indeed, the ones who participate in the two resurrections will be as different as heaven and hell. That is why very separate fates are required in eternity. Heaven is a prepared place for a prepared people. Hell and the Lake of Fire are prepared for unprepared people!

8 | Will Any Believers Be on the Earth After the Rapture and During the Tribulation?

What a difference a day makes! One day: all the preserving, healing, helping influence of Christians still being felt throughout the world. The next day: all good influence totally absent—gone from government, gone from business, gone from homes, gone from education. One day: errands of mercy, acts of compassion, expressions of love still going on. The next day: the needs of the world met with depraved indifference. One day: millions of earnest and tender-hearted believers trying their best to help lost souls find the Kingdom of God through their Lord Jesus Christ. The next day: a lost man saying, "No man careth for my soul."

EVERY BELIEVER CAUGHT AWAY

The difference? The abrupt departure of the Church at the return of Christ. The Rapture!

"Rapture" is from the Latin "rapio," meaning to snatch or remove away suddenly. "Rapture" implies "carrying away to sublime happiness." It is a post-biblical word used by Christians to indicate the "catching up" of the Church to heaven. As surely as Philip was caught away literally and physically, and the Ethiopian convert saw him no more (Acts 8:39), so all the believers will be caught away (1 Thessalonians 4:17) and the world will see them no more! In the twinkling of an eye (a split-second movement), it will have happened and the Christians of the world will be gone (1 Corinthians 15:52).

Many will be left behind in that sudden transition of the Church (Luke 17:34–36). All that will be left behind will be those who are unsaved and therefore unprepared for the Rapture. This means that at first, only unbelievers will populate the earth following the Rapture. The Scriptures teach that a horrible period of history will then ensue (Matthew 24:21; Isaiah 65:12–15; 66:15, 16; Daniel 12:1; Revelation 6). What makes it such a terrible time of trouble is the fact that the Christians, who have been holding the line against absolute evil, will depart.

THE HOLY SPIRIT'S MINISTRY
CHANGED

The believers' bodies have been the temple of the Holy Ghost (2 Thessalonians 2:6–8; 1 Corinthians 6:19). After the intense Church-age activity of the Holy Spirit ceases (John 6:63, 65; 14:17, 26; 16:8, 13; 2 Thessalonians 2:7), it will be extremely difficult for a person to have faith to believe the Gospel (2 Thessalonians 2:11, 12). The Holy Spirit has always been present in the world. Many passages of the Old Testament speak of the work of the Holy Spirit (Numbers 11:17; Nehemiah 9:20; Job 32:8; Psalms 51:11). We are told by Stephen in Acts 7:51 that the Old Testament Jews resisted that work. We also learn in 2 Peter 1:21 that it was the moving of the Holy Spirit that caused the Old Testament Scriptures to be written.

At Pentecost the Holy Spirit came in a special fullness to the Church. To this same extent, He will be taken out of the world with the Rapture of the Church. After that, the demonic forces of Satan will move out into the world almost unhindered. The antichrist will be revealed and will deceive many (Matthew 24:5; 2 Thessalonians 2:4, 9, 10); but God will continue to save those who come to Him in the name of Jesus Christ, as He has in other ages. During the final stages of history, God will move on to save souls as He did in the beginning of history. He is "longsuffering to us—ward, not willing that any should perish, but that all should come to repentance" (2 Peter 3:9).

ANTICHRIST REVEALED

By a careful study of Revelation 11:1, 2, and Daniel 9:24–27, we conclude that the antichrist will be revealed shortly after the Rapture, arising as a great architect of peace out of the "sea" or confusion resulting from the Rapture. He will reign over the world for a period of seven years. The first three and one-half years will be characterized by peace and prosperity. The last three and one-half years, however, will be characterized by great tribulation. This last period is the same forty-two months mentioned in Revelation 11:2. At the beginning of this last half of the seven-year period, or, "in the midst of a week," as Daniel puts it, the antichrist breaks a covenant with the Jews and sets an idol of himself in their national temple. This will be the beginning of the antichrist's persecution of the Jewish people—a period called by Daniel the "time of trouble" (Daniel 12:1). This is God's way of chastising his people, purging them of sin and unbelief (Zechariah 13:9).

JEWS EVANGELIZED AND SAVED

During the last part of the antichrist's reign, the Jews will recognize Christ as their true Messiah (Zechariah 12:10; 13:1) and be saved. At this time, 144,000 Jewish evangelists will be sent throughout the world. (Read Revelation 7.) There, the angels of God are about to loose the winds of God's wrath upon the earth. But God commands by another angel that nothing be done until 144,000 Jews are sealed. The word "seal" means "reserve in protective keeping." In olden days, it also meant an identifying mark. In this passage it means both. They will be divinely protected from all that the antichrist will try to do to them. None of the great natural catastrophes described in the opening of the seals in chapter 6 will hurt them. They will have the "everlasting Gospel" to preach, and will carry it to all nations (Revelation 14:6). Many more Jews will be converted, and multitudes of Gentiles (Revelation 7:9, 14). Conversion in those days will be costly. The price will be the sacrifice of one's life for his faith. The antichrist will put those who follow Christ to death, probably in the most cruel manner (Revelation 6:9–11; 13:7, 15). But regardless of the imminence of martyrdom, so many are saved that their number is beyond man's ability to count (Revelation 7:9). They refuse to receive the mark of the Beast (Revelation 13:16–

18; 14:9–11) and instead wear proudly the name of their Lord stamped on their foreheads (Revelation 9:4; 14:1). Later on, when God unleashes His judgments on the followers of antichrist, that "seal" on the foreheads of believers will protect them during the five months of terror and torture by an army of demons (Revelation 9:1–11).

BELIEVERS WILL SURVIVE TRIBULATION

Most of the ones who are saved as a result of the witness of the 144,000 evangelists will be immediately killed, but some will survive. The many who have gone into hiding in the mountains (Matthew 24:15–22) at the beginning of the antichrist's persecution will survive. The 144,000 divinely protected evangelists will survive. These believers will greet the Lord and the saints from heaven when the Lord returns to end the Battle of Armageddon at the close of the Tribulation period (Matthew 24:29, 30; Zechariah 14:3; Revelation 19:11–15).

These living believers will be the only mortal humans who will begin the Kingdom age; having the capacity of reproduction, they will re-people the earth. All other human beings (the unbelievers left after the destruction of that final world war) will be judged and destroyed (Matthew 25:46).

The martyred saints will be raised at the Second Coming and join those who were raised in the first phase of the first Resurrection. (The two parts complete the "first Resurrection" mentioned in Revelation 20.) Together, they will reign with Christ a thousand years (Revelation 20:4–6). These resurrected saints will have their perfect, glorified bodies and will be able to travel back and forth between heaven and earth and throughout God's creation (1 John 3:2; 1 Corinthians 2:9; Romans 8:29; John 1:12; Job 1:6; 2:1).

IT WOULD BE BETTER NOW

The answer to the question of our chapter title is an emphatic "yes!" People *will* believe and be saved after the Rapture of the New Testament Church, but at great price. Believers will live through the Tribulation period, but in great suffering.

The question that comes to mind in the light of all this is, "Why run a risk like that at all?" This is the Gospel age. Invitations to Christ are everywhere. The best time, the easiest time to be saved is now (Hebrews 4:7; 2 Corinthians 6:2). Consider this: if you have difficulty coming to Christ now with so much to help you, it is most likely that in the Tribulation period you will not be able to come at all. Yes, after the Rapture, there will be believers. But if you have already heard the Gospel and have not been able to surrender to Christ now, you certainly should not hope to be a believer then. Right now is the time to be saved if you are not already saved. "Behold, I stand at the door and knock . . ." (Revelation 3:20).

9 | What Is Meant By "The Last Trump"?

From the very earliest days of human history, the sound of the trumpet has been a signal of importance. Preceding processions of royalty, blasting out battle calls, or heralding the homecoming of heroes, the trumpet blast was always a sound that demanded attention. Trumpets will sound in the Rapture.

PREVIOUS TRUMPETS

"At the last trump" is a phrase occuring in 1 Corinthians 15:52. It is a figure of speech borrowed from the military life of Bible days. As an army prepared for action, three trumpets were sounded. The first was the command for the men to gather their gear and put on their armor. The second was a command to form the marching formation. When the "last trump" was sounded, it was the signal for the army to move out (Numbers 10:6, 9)!

The expression is used in 1 Corinthians 15:52 to denote that the first and second trumpets have already sounded, and that the Rapture is so imminent that we need only listen for the last trumpet.

Historically speaking, the advent of the Gospel Age with John the Baptist preaching in the wilderness was the first trumpet (Matthew 11:9, 10; Luke 16:16). The second trumpet was the giving of charismatic credentials to the Christian Church on the day of Pentecost (Acts 2:16–21). These two "trumpets" were prophesied as special signals (Malachi 3:1; Joel 2:28). They have served to call all men to be clothed in the armor of Christ's righteousness and to fall into the formation of the visible Church. Now, the Church awaits the signal to move to heaven!

Spiritually speaking, the first trumpet sounds when a lost soul feels God calling him to be saved and to put on the "whole armor of God" (Ephesians 6:13). The second trumpet is the immediate call of the Spirit which tells a new convert to identify with the Church and its work. He then is to live in alert anticipation of the "last trump."

But the idea captured here in the language of the Apostle Paul is that when the "last trump" sounds, we will move out without any further delay! The twin events of the Resurrection and the Rapture of the saints wait only for the authorized signal.

A NOTE OF VICTORY

The Resurrection will begin with the blast of trumpets and the shout of God. The first inkling that the Day of Days is at hand will be sounds from the skies that have never before been heard on earth!

Unsaved and unregenerated people will not be equipped with the kind of hearing necessary to hear and respond to this signal, but it will be a penetrating sound to every believer (John 10:27). There are graves so deep that uninterrupted silence has reigned in them since the day the bodies were left there. But the sound of the trumpet will be heard—down in the mine shafts, down in the wreckage of ships on the ocean floor! The bodies of believers will be raised all over the planet (Isaiah 26:19), and there will be a new order of life in those new bodies. The new bodies will no longer be susceptible to disease. Never again will a cough or a groan be heard. No aches, allergies, or ailments of any sort! No deformities, defects, or disabilities! Never again will there be a need for hospitals, drug stores, or funeral homes. Gone forever will be the need for such things as eyeglasses, false teeth, crutches, braces, or wheelchairs! We will then be free from the "former things of earth" (Revelation 21:4). Think of what a victory that will be! Gladly will I give up this weak, sin-infested frame to the grave knowing it soon will be given back uncorrupted and immortal at the sound of the last trumpet (1 Corinthians 15:54)!

A SUDDEN CHANGE

Here is something truly sensational! We will not all die. Those believers living on the earth at the time of the last trumpet will simply be changed into people with immortal bodies (1 Corinthians 15:51). In 1 Corinthians 15:52, both the resurrection and the translation are mentioned: "The *dead* shall be raised incorruptible, and *we* shall be changed." God has given us two previews of the translation that will occur at the time of the last trumpet: Enoch (Genesis 5:24; Hebrews 11:5) and Elijah (2 Kings 2:11). As Enoch suddenly "was not," so our own disappearance from this earth will be abrupt and sudden. As Elijah was caught up and away and could not be found, so we will be.

THE NEXT EVENT

The sound of the trumpet will be heard very soon. This page of history is about to be turned. While many predicted events are between us and the appearing of Christ in the glorious Second Coming, nothing at all lies between us and the Rapture. According to the Word of God, the testimony of the Lord Jesus, and the united testimony of the Apostles, there is not even the thickness of tissue paper between us and the events brought forth by the sound of the final trumpet! (Matthew 24:44–51; James 5:7–9).

According to 1 Thessalonians 5:4, we should not let the suddenness of the Rapture catch us unprepared. And in Romans 13:11, 12, we are warned that it is "high time that we awake out of sleep." We ought to be listening for the trumpet! It is past time to take up the "armor of light"—*that* trumpet has sounded for us already. You ought to be saved already. It is past time for us to "fall in" the formation of an organized church—we have heard *that* trumpet already. Now, we should be faithfully listening for the "last trumpet!" Listen! I can almost hear it now: that "voice as the sound of many waters" (Revelation 1:15) with which Jesus shouts for the dead to come forth (1 Thessalonians 4:16; John 11:43); that voice of the archangel and his legions of angels from the far end of heaven (Isaiah 13:5); and that crystal-clear clarion call of God's trumpet! Look! The heavens are opening up! What a choir! What angelic music! What beautiful light! And what stirring trumpet-notes! Hush! Listen, oh, listen to the trumpet!

To order additional copies or to arrange for speaking engagements write to the author at Post Office Box 331, Redan, Georgia, 30074.

**WHEREVER PAPERBACKS ARE SOLD
OR USE THIS COUPON**

 Whitaker House

504 LAUREL DRIVE
MONROEVILLE, PA 15146

**SEND INSPIRATIONAL BOOKS
LISTED BELOW**

Title	Price	
		☐ Send Complete Catalog
_____	____	
_____	____	
_____	____	
_____	____	
_____	____	
_____	____	
_____	____	

Name_____

Street_____

City_____State_____Zip____

Suggested Inspirational Paperback Books

FACE UP WITH A MIRACLE $1.25
  by Don Basham

> This is a fascinating book about God the Holy
> Spirit bringing a new dimension into the lives
> of twentieth-century Christians. It is filled with
> experiences that testify to a God of miracles
> being unleashed in our lives right now.

**BAPTISM IN THE HOLY SPIRIT: COMMAND OR
OPTION?   by Bob Campbell** $1.25

> A teaching summary on the Holy Spirit, cov-
> ering the three kinds of baptisms, the various
> workings of the Holy Spirit, the question of
> tongues and how to know when you have re-
> ceived the Baptism of the Spirit.

**A SCRIPTURAL OUTLINE OF THE BAPTISM IN
THE HOLY SPIRIT   by George and
Harriet Gillies**   60¢

> Here is a very brief and simple outline of the
> Baptism in the Holy Spirit, with numerous
> references under each point. This handy little
> booklet is a good reference for any question
> you might have concerning this subject.

A HANDBOOK ON HOLY SPIRIT BAPTISM $1.25
  by Don Basham

> Questions and answers on the Baptism in the
> Holy Spirit and speaking in tongues. The book
> is in great demand, and answers many impor-
> tant questions from within the contemporary
> Christian Church.

HE SPOKE, AND I WAS STRENGTHENED $1.25
by Dick Mills

An easy-to-read devotional of 52 prophetic scripturally-based messages directed to the businessman, the perfectionist, the bereaved, the lonely, the ambitious and many more.

SEVEN TIMES AROUND $1.25
by Bob and Ruth McKee

A Christian growth story of a family who receives the Baptism in the Holy Spirit and then applies this new experience to solve the family's distressing, but frequently humorous problems.

LET GO!   95¢
by Fenelon

Jesus promised a life full of joy and peace. Why then are so many Christians struggling to attain the qualities that Christ said belonged to the child of God? Fenelon speaks firmly— but lovingly to those whose lives have been an up hill battle. Don't miss this one.

VISIONS BEYOND THE VEIL   95¢
by H. A. Baker

Beggar children who heard the Gospel at a rescue mission in China, received a powerful visitation of the Holy Spirit, during which they saw visions of heaven and Christ which cannot be explained away. A new revised edition.

DEAR DAD, THIS IS TO ANNOUNCE MY DEATH $1.25
by Ric Kast

The story of how rock music, drugs and alcohol lead a youth to commit suicide. While Ric waits out the last moments of life, Jesus Christ rescues him from death and gives him a new life.

GATEWAY TO POWER $1.25
by Wesley Smith

From the boredom of day after day routine and lonely nights of meaningless activity, Wes Smith was caught up into a life of miracles. Dramatic healings, remarkable financial assistance, and exciting escapes from dangerous situations have become part of his life.

SIGI AND I 95¢
by Gwen Schmidt

The intriguing narration of how two women smuggled Bibles and supplies to Christians behind the Iron Curtain. An impressive account of their simple faith in following the Holy Spirit.

MINISTERING THE BAPTISM
IN THE HOLY SPIRIT   by Don Basham $1.00

Over 100 received their Baptism after hearing the author give this important message. The book deals with such topics as the Baptism as a second experience, the primary evidence of the Baptism, and tongues and the "chronic seeker."

THE LAST CHAPTER $1.25
by A. W. Rasmussen

An absorbing narrative based on the author's own experience, in the charismatic renewal around the world. He presents many fresh insights on fasting, church discipline and Christ's Second Coming.

A HANDBOOK ON TONGUES, INTERPRETATION
AND PROPHECY   by Don Basham $1.25

The second of Don Basham's handbook series. Again set up in the convenient question and answer format, the book addresses itself to further questions on the Holy Spirit, especially the vocal gifts.